★★★★★

MLB TEAMS

Los Angeles ANGELS

KENNY ABDO

Fly!
An Imprint of Abdo Zoom
abdobooks.com

abdobooks.com

Published by Abdo Zoom, a division of ABDO, P.O. Box 398166, Minneapolis, Minnesota 55439.

Printed in the United States of America, North Mankato, Minnesota.
102025
012026

THIS BOOK CONTAINS RECYCLED MATERIALS

Photo Credits: Getty Images, Shutterstock
Production Contributors: Kenny Abdo, Jennie Forsberg, Grace Hansen
Design Contributors: Candice Keimig, Neil Klinepier

Library of Congress Control Number: 2025936781

Publisher's Cataloging-in-Publication Data

Names: Abdo, Kenny, author.
Title: Los Angeles Angels / by Kenny Abdo
Description: Minneapolis, Minnesota : Abdo Zoom, 2026 | Series: MLB teams | Includes online resources and index.
Identifiers: ISBN 9798384940210 (lib. bdg.) | ISBN 9798384940975 (ebook) | ISBN 9798384941354 (read-to-me ebook)
Subjects: LCSH: Los Angeles Angels (Baseball team)--Juvenile literature. | Baseball teams--Juvenile literature. | Professional sports--Juvenile literature. | Sports franchises--Juvenile literature. | Major League Baseball (Organization)--Juvenile literature.
Classification: DDC 796.357--dc23

Table of CONTENTS

ANGELS

Since 1961, the Los Angeles Angels have brought big hits and hometown pride, making Southern California (SoCal) feel like a little slice of heaven!

GEICO
FIELD

ANGELS
27

With star players like Mike Trout in the lineup, the team shines brightly in the City of Angels.

BATTER UP!

The Los Angeles Angels formed in 1961. The team began play in the expanding **American League** (**AL**), giving SoCal baseball fans another team to root for.

NGELES

The Angels played their first season at Wrigley Field in Los Angeles. From 1962 to 1965, the Angels and the Dodgers shared Dodger Stadium. In 1966, the Angels moved to Angel Stadium in Anaheim. The ballpark's famous Big A sign still stands today.

NGELS

The Angels had some great moments, but struggled to win games at first. Fans hoped for better days ahead as the team grew.

GRAND SLAMS

Nolan Ryan joined the Angels in 1972 and quickly became a star. His powerful pitching helped put the team on the map, giving fans a lot to cheer for!

The Angels won their first **division** title in 1979, finishing with 88 wins. Don Baylor led the team with 36 home runs and won the **AL** MVP award. He helped the Angels prove they could compete with the best!

KENNEDY

In 2002, the Angels went to the World Series in an all-California matchup against the San Francisco Giants. After a thrilling seven-game series, the Angels swarmed **closer** Troy Percival after the final out to win!

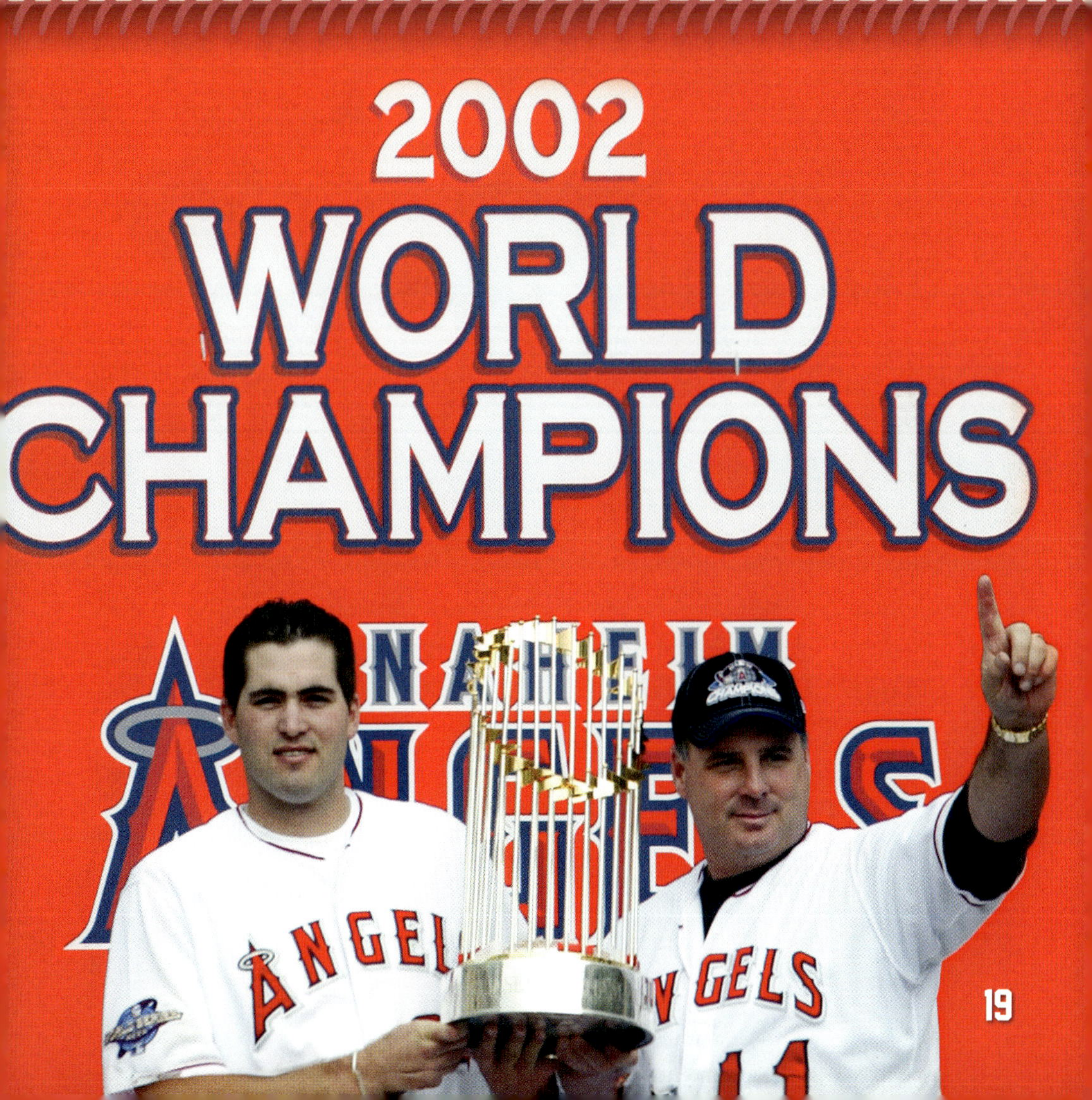

In the years that followed, the Angels continued to stack the roster with solid players. Top performers like Albert Pujols, Jared Weaver, and Mike Trout brought excitement to the field.

Trout
ANGELS
5

Right-handed pitcher and left-handed slugger Shohei Ohtani arrived to Los Angeles from Japan in 2018. He chose the Angels over six other teams. He burst onto the scene, winning the **AL Rookie** of the Year award.

Even with a solid lineup through 2025, team success was hard to come by. The Angels hoped that having great players, like Trout and Taylor Ward, would eventually lead to another championship run.

HALL OF FAME

Jim Edmonds brought electricity to the field with his amazing catches and clutch hitting for the Angels from 1993 to 2000. He was a three-time **All-Star** and won two **Gold Gloves**. Edmonds also crushed 121 home runs for the Angels and recorded 43 outfield assists, showing off his strong arm and skills.

Mike Trout has been the face of the Angels since his debut in 2011. He is a three-time MVP and 11-time **All-Star** with 389 home runs and more than 200 stolen bases. Trout has also won nine Silver Slugger Awards. With his great catches and strong leadership, he ranks among the best to ever wear an Angels uniform.

Shohei Ohtani dazzled Angels fans from 2018 to 2023. He hit 171 home runs, recorded 437 **RBIs**, stole 58 bases, and posted a .274 batting average in 701 games. On the mound, he earned a 38–19 **record**, struck out 608 batters over 481⅔ innings, and posted a 3.01 **ERA**. Ohtani made history in 2021 as being selected to an **All-Star** team as both a pitcher and a hitter!

GLOSSARY

All-Star – an athlete named to the yearly baseball contest, called the All-Star Game, where top players from the AL and the National League (NL) compete against each other.

American League (AL) – one of two 15-team leagues that make up MLB.

closer – a specialized relief pitcher who enters the game in the late innings.

division – a number of teams grouped together in a sport for competitive purposes.

Earned-Run Average (ERA) – the average number of earned runs per game scored against a pitcher.

Gold Glove Award – an annual award given to the best fielders at each position in both the AL and NL.

record – the combined total of a pitcher's wins and losses in a season.

rookie – a professional athlete in his or her first season in a sport.

Runs Batted In (RBI) – a statistic that credits a batter for making a play that allows a run to be scored.

ONLINE RESOURCES

Booklinks
NONFICTION NETWORK
FREE! ONLINE NONFICTION RESOURCES

To learn more about the Los Angeles Angels, please visit **abdobooklinks.com** or scan this QR code. These links are routinely monitored and updated to provide the most current information available.

INDEX